Tabitha Fink

and the Cowboy Code

by Rick Felty

tabithafink.com

hi

ISBN-13 978-0-984052738
ISBN-10 0984052739

Printed in the United States of America.

Published by Dreamschooner Press.

www.dreamschoonerpress.com

For Mary O'Baidy, a woman who lived her life like Tabitha Fink;
embracing adventure, making new friends
and having the courage to be herself.

I am Tabitha Fink,
the cat with one eye,
and I like to try things
no other cats try.

Although I seem different,
I'm happy to be,
the one and true Tabitha Fink...
that is me.

So listen my friends
to a story that's true.
It's starting right now,
and I wrote it for you.

I am Tabitha Fink,
a wild western cat.
And I live in this town,
and I wear
this big hat.

I'm the sheriff round here,
with a star on my vest.
Keeping everyone safe,
always trying my best.

My deputy here
is Bartholomew Blink
He's brave and he's helpful,
just like you would think.

He's quick on the draw,
with a crayon of course.
And he wears a blue hat
and rides a small horse.

The people who live here
are right friendly folk.
They're kind to each other,
and quick with a joke.

They have many jobs.
They all do their part.
But somewhere inside,
they're all cowboys
at heart.

The blacksmith in town
is important to all.
She tends to our horses.
She's there when we call.

Without her I just
don't know what
we would do,
when each of
our horses,
might need a
new shoe.

This is the barber,
who fixes our hair.
He snips with precision,
he styles with great care.

But there's
something he does,
that is really quite dear.
We tell him our troubles
and he lends us an ear.

Our teacher helps all of the kids
learn in school.
From reading to math,
they study
each rule.

When they make a mistake
she knows it's OK.
It's all part of learning,
just finding their way.

This cowboy he rides for the Pony Express.
It's how we do mail here in the wild west.

He jumps on his horse
with the letters we write
and delivers our words,
by day and by night.

Life in this town was quite peaceful and sweet, when one day a stranger walked down our main street...

... with his horse,
who seemed tired.
The man looked a bit scary.
He wore a big hat,
and his face was real hairy.

"Good morning kind sir,"
I said to the man.
"I am Tabitha Fink, can I let you a hand?"

"This town you are in
is quite friendly and nice.
I can show you around,
you don't have to ask twice."

"I am Ornery the Outlaw,
the name I go by.
I'm mean as can be.
And you wanna know why?"

"Cause I don't have a friend,
that's true, it's no jest.
It's just me and my horse,
in the lonesome Wild West."

"Well here in our town, perhaps you would find that having new friends would bring peace of mind."

"You need not be
ornery, though
that IS your
name.
But having no
friends would
be quite
a shame!"

"I had a good friend once,
but we had a fight.
Now years have gone by,
and I can't make it right."

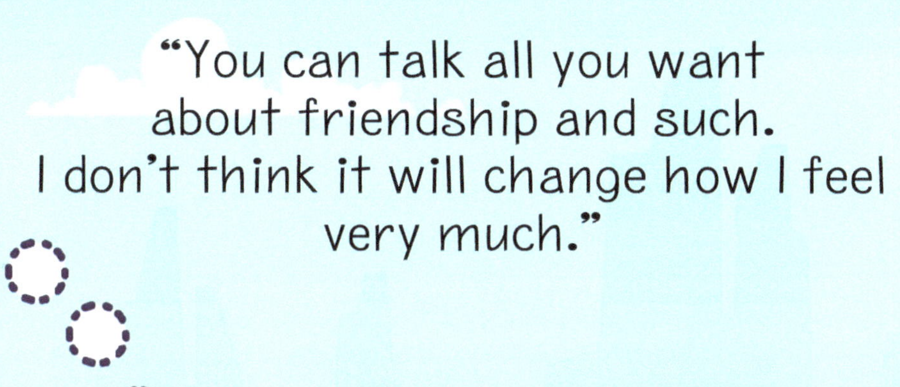
"You can talk all you want
about friendship and such.
I don't think it will change how I feel
very much."

"There are other things too,
besides just no friends.
The itching I feel from this beard
never ends!"

"And I can't seem to add up
the gold in my pack
since math is another life skill
that I lack."

"But I am fine without friends,
I don't need your advice.
As I told you before,
I am not very nice."

"Now leave me alone!"
he said with a frown.
"Or I'll steal all the money
you have in this town!"

"Good friends are a great thing
that life has to give,"
said Bartholomew Blink.
"It's the best way to live."

"Let Tabitha Fink
show you how it can be,
to have friends in your life,
and then you will see."

They walked to the blacksmith,
the horse came along.
The smithy was working
and singing a song.

“Hello Tabitha Fink
and Bartholomew too.
I believe I can tell
that this horse needs a shoe.”

"This is our friend,
Mister Outlaw,"
said Fink.
"You're right, his horse
needs a new shoe
I should think."

“I will fix him up fast,”
said the blacksmith
“of course!”
“I’ll help this nice friend
and his friendly nice horse.”

Outlaw asked, “Why
would you want to help me?
I’m not very nice.
I’m as mean as can be.”

"But thanks for the help,
it means quite a lot.
My horse will feel better,
all ready to trot."

When the horse was all set,
they walked down the street
to the shop where the barber
was waving to greet.

"Hello my good pals,"
said the barber with cheer.
"Who is this new friend
you have with you here?"

"Mister Outlaw,"
said Tabitha Fink with a grin.
"He is new to our town,
can you please fit him in?"

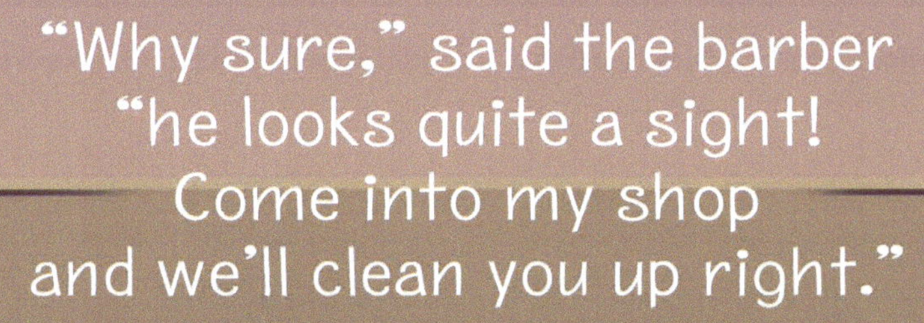

"Why sure," said the barber
"he looks quite a sight!
Come into my shop
and we'll clean you up right."

A half hour later,
the two men appeared.
"I feel great," said the Outlaw,
"without my old beard."

"I'm happy to help,"
said the barber with glee.
"Now spread this good cheer
to all that you see."

"Maybe I shouldn't
decide that I'm mean,"
thought Ornery the Outlaw,
"after all that I've seen."

"I'm starting to get how far
kindness can go
when you help other people
with things that you know."

Just then the
school teacher
came by on her way.
“Hello Tabitha Fink.
Good to see you
today.”

"It is such
a nice thing,
you should
happen on by,"
said Tabitha Fink,
a gleam in her eye.

"My friend here says
math is too hard
to compute.
He can't seem to add up
his sacks full of loot."

"I wonder if you could
just show him the way,
to count all the gold
that he gets every day."

"Math can be tricky,
but I'll help him to see,
that math can be fun,
just take it from me."

"We'll go to the school,
I won't keep him late.
He'll know his math facts,
sure as nine follows eight."

That afternoon
when he came back
from school
Mister Outlaw said,
"who knew that
math was so cool?"

"I now know addition, to add up my gold.
I love this math stuff. It'll never get old!"

"I love my friends too,
they are friendly indeed.
It is nice to have help
with the things that I need."

"I just wish my old friend
would get back in touch.
I miss our old chats,
I miss them so much."

Just then a fast horse
galloped right into town.

Whoooosh!!!

The rider jumped off,
began looking around.

"Hello Tabitha Fink
and Bartholomew too.
I'm holding a message,
but it isn't for you."

"It's the Pony Express,
hello there young man.

Tell us the name
and we'll do what we can.

We'll find the right person
for that special letter.

We know the whole town,
no one knows this town
better."

Mr.
Outlaw

"It says Mister Outlaw,
but that can't be right.
This town is so friendly,
no one here likes to fight
or to steal or be mean
or to act like a bully.

There aren't Outlaw's here,
I know this town fully!"

"Wait," said Bartholomew,
"here's the man that you seek!
He's Ornery the Outlaw,
hasn't been here a week.

But he's made many friends
since he walked through our door.
He must be the one that your letter is for."

He looked at the letter,
and wanted to squeal.
Then both eyes went wide,
like an old wagon wheel.

"Well bless every tumbleweed
and all that is dusty.
This letter is from
my best dear-old-friend

Rusty!"

Then Ornery the Outlaw
read the words Rusty wrote.
And after,
he shared all the thoughts in the note.

"He says he is sorry
for the fight that we had.
He's spent all this time
feeling lonely and sad."

"He heard I was here
in this kind western town.
So he gathered his thoughts
and wrote them all down."

"Said he is focused on joy
and not sorrow..."

"And he's catching a stagecoach. He'll be here..."

"Tomorrow!!"

“This is great news,” cried Tabitha Fink.
“We’ll plan a big hoedown, as quick as a wink.
To celebrate Rusty, and all your new friends.
With happy beginnings instead of sad ends.”

Outlaw

The next day
the stagecoach
arrived in the town.
With Ornery and friends
all gathered around.

Down the very short steps
came a man with red hair,
who wore fancy boots
and a hat with great flair.

"It's so nice,"
said Rusty "to see
you again.
A treasure for sure,
to have a good friend."

"I know what you mean," said the Outlaw with glee. "So great we're together, my friend Rusty and me!"

"I've learned so much here
in this wonderful town,"
said Ornery the Outlaw looking around.

"All of you people have helped me to see that life can be happier than I thought it could be."

So the whole town came out,
for a western hoedown.
And when Tabitha spoke,
they all gathered 'round.

"To all our good friends
from near and from far,
we're happy you're here,
whoever you are!"

"My new friend the Outlaw,
once thought he was mean.
But the good parts of life,
he hadn't yet seen."

"When the blacksmith,
the barber and teacher
took part,
he learned all the
goodness he has
in his heart."

"The kindness and friendship you townsfolk all showed is what we all know as the true Cowboy Code."

"We practice it here
in the open wild west.
By helping each other,
we're all at our best."

"So be kind to your friends,
even friends you don't know.
And help others out,
wherever you go."

"Friendship and kindness
can make the world great.
Please try them right now,
there's no reason to wait."

bye

Rick Felty lives in New England
with his wonderful family and lots of pets.

Visit

tabithafink.com

AND you can see a picture of the real Tabitha Fink
and learn more about why she only had one eye.

Also available in the Award-Winning Tabitha Fink Series

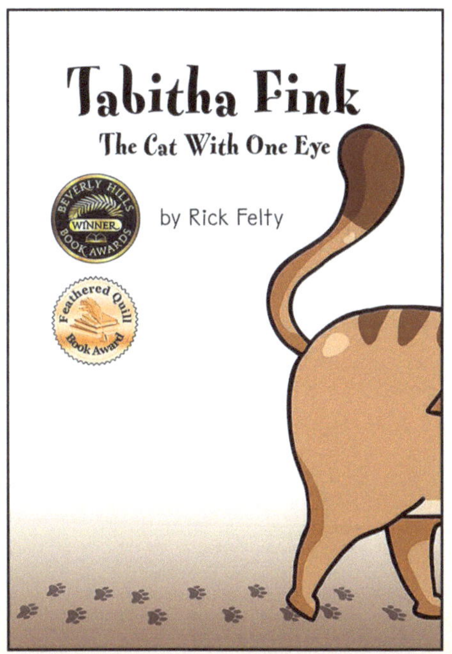

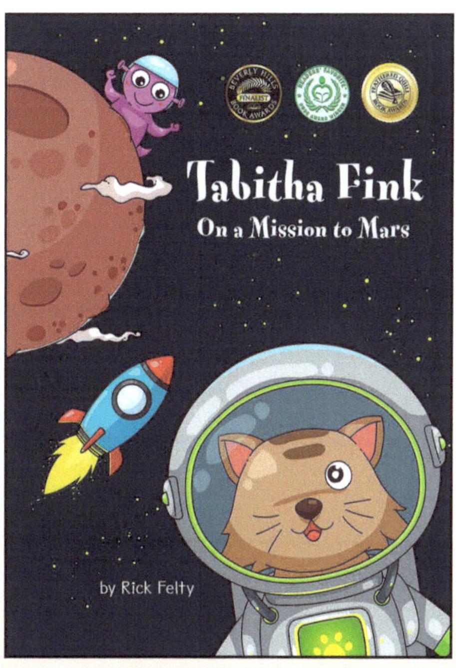

www.ingramcontent.com/pod-product-compliance
Lightning Source LLC
LaVergne TN
LVHW070133110826
845147LV00002B/245

* 9 7 8 0 9 8 4 0 5 2 7 3 8 *